Prune & Prosper

Abundant Fruit Through
Empowered Stewardship

Daniel F. Sciortino, ChFC®

First Printing, 2020

ISBN 9798634583648

www.FigTreeStewardship.com

Dedication

I dedicate this book to my dad who sacrificed and took risks for our family. May the fruit that this book produces be a testimony to the seeds of faith you have planted in our lives.

TABLE OF CONTENTS

Acknowledgements

I first want to thank my wife for her support. She is not a risk taker but gives me the green light when she knows God is calling me to do something. When things are uncertain and I get stuck, she reminds me to release control. This book would've taken much longer to write if she didn't keep the kids busy at times during the process. My three children always inspire me to be a better person and to bring out the kid in me. I hope this book inspires them to not only create, but to put the little things that God gives them back in His hands, and watch Him multiply.

My parents have always provided for me to follow my dreams and fostered the environment for it. My brother has been a huge help in my endcavors and always reminds me to have fun in the process. My sister will always make the journey better with her loving encouragement and texts with heart emojis.

This whole book journey started when God watered the seed for me to write this book through Rev. Marsha Mansour when I bumped into her at a local restaurant. A special thank you to Pastor Chris Morante for his counsel, prayers and sermon on "dreaming dreams again." I also sincerely appreciate all of my social media friends and followers for their likes, comments and shares. Thank you to all of my clients for letting me into their world and trusting me with their finances.

Most of all, I want to thank God for His grace and patience with me. I'm just a rusty tool made useful with His oil.

Introduction

I knew I was called to write this book for such a time as this. What I didn't realize was that weeks after I finished writing the first draft, our nation and world was going to be rattled by the Coronavirus outbreak. Unsure about whether this was a smart business decision to launch this book during an outbreak and struggling economy, I prayed for direction. That same week I attended an online business networking group meeting and a minister in the group shared his thoughts with the group and said, "I feel like God is pruning us right now". "Our lives, routines, finances and comforts have been disrupted." I truly believe this book will not only inspire people in these difficult times, but it will help them rebuild and bear more fruit when we rise out of this season.

This book will take you through a journey of pruning inspired by a fig tree I tended to for many years.

I will walk you through ways to prune your investments through biblically responsible investing, your finances, your time and various aspects of your life so you can start to bear fruit or bear more fruit than you already are. All of the principles and ideas you will read will have a biblical foundation and my hope is that you will become an empowered steward of what God has blessed you with. Through empowered stewardship, we can truly prosper. I'm not talking about what the world calls prosperity. I'm talking about contentment in God's blessings and abundance, true wealth, joy from blessing others, freedom from the grip of money and debt, expanded territory, fruit of the Spirit, balance and riches in Heaven. Get your pruning shears ready and read with an open heart.

When God called me, I said, "Here I Am Lord". So... here I am. What do you say?

Chapter 1

Purpose of Pruning

My deep dive into the art of pruning came about after my wife Tara and I purchased our first home a few months before getting married. We purchased our home before getting married because we wanted to renovate and furnish the home and have it ready for when we returned from our honeymoon. Once the renovations to the interior of our home were complete, we turned our attention to the backyard. There, we noticed the perfect spot to plant a fruit tree. But what kind of tree should we plant? We both loved figs and had always heard about all their health benefits, in addition to being a cool and mysterious ancient fruit mentioned in the Bible. So, I decided to plant a small fig tree, purchased from a local nursery. I didn't realize at the time what I was getting myself into as it turned out to be ten years of wrestling with this tree for a good harvest. I learned how to plant it; how to prepare the soil; how to position for maximum sun exposure; how not to over water it; how to protect it for the winter months; and lastly, how to prune it. Year after year, I watered, over watered, pruned, pruned again, pruned too much and pruned too little. Did I mention pruning? You see, fig trees go from dormant in the winter to just exploding with leaves and new branches in the spring and summer. Pruning is essential in their care. Eventually the tree grew to be taller than me and very wide. Covering it for the winter months became an hour-long process of not only wrapping it perfectly, but also making sure I used the right material to control the moisture level. One fall, I remember wrapping the tree up and joyfully thinking to myself, "this summer, we are finally going to get a ton of figs!". However, somehow the frost made its way into my nicely wrapped bundle of fig joy, and killed half of the branches. I essentially had to cut all those branches off and practically start all over again. Every year I thought I had the process down. But each spring, I realized that something else had gone wrong.

Now, you may have travelled to Sicily or Israel and have seen massive unattended wild fig trees with a ton of fruit. If they were to be pruned, they would bear even more fruit. That's because they are where they belong, in the perfect climate and environment without harsh winters (unlike my little fig tree planted in Northern New Jersey). These trees naturally get the right amount of rain, wind, sun and are already in ideal soil. Northern New Jersey is not the optimal environment for them to thrive. In my learning process, however, I came across a gentleman that had migrated from Italy. He lived in a town nearby and never covered his fig tree in the winter. Somehow his fig tree survived and thrived. I came to learn that it had something to do with the radiant heat coming off of the side of his house from the sun as well as being tucked in a nice spot sheltered from the wind. This really reinforced the fact that the further away a tree is from where it can thrive, the more attention and pruning needs to be done.

Fast forward ten years, and the time came to once again uncover our fig tree in the spring time. After unwrapping all the layers and removing the pile of dried leaves I used to help insulate it from the cold, I was thrilled to see that the tree survived the winter! Not one branch had died from the wintery frost. I thought to myself, again, "this is the year I'm finally gonna eat an abundance of figs." Up until that season, we had only eaten a handful of figs over the ten years. I was so inspired and determined that I pruned like a true master, as if I had ten hands. I watered it just the right amount. I even talked to it. Sure enough, by July the tree exploded with growth of new branches, leaves and a ton of figlets! This was definitely the year.

August rolled around and typically if my fig tree had borne any fruit, it was by the end of this month that the figs would normally ripen. But these figs were staying the same size and not ripening. Since my hopes were dashed for an August harvest, I started to hope for a hot September. If not, these figs would stay the same size and never ripen. Figs aren't like a banana where you can pick them in the green stage and then they ripen on your counter. If you pick a fig before it is ripe, it won't ripen on its own. It just withers and rots. It must remain on the tree to ripen.

We were blessed with a hot September and the figs got bigger but still not fully ripe. I picked a few to see if they were edible, but they weren't. Now mid-September was upon us and here I am with another mystery to solve. What was going on? I thought I had done everything right. If the fall chill came, these figs were never going to ripen and just die right on the tree. Here I am with a tree full of figs but unable to eat or share one. I was so frustrated for various reasons. I was frustrated not only because of the hard work and hopes I had put into this tree for years, but also because it was reminding me of aspects of my life. I began to reflect on how it seemed like a lot of my efforts were either bearing very little fruit or just never ripening into anything meaningful. I knew it was time for some serious pruning of my life and to ask God to reveal areas I was unaware that needed pruning. I was reminded of this verse:

"He cuts off every branch in me that bears no fruit, while every branch that does bear fruit he prunes so that it will be even more fruitful."
John 15:2

These powerful words became the foundational Bible verse for this book and my life.

In the next chapter, I will describe what was a breakthrough not only for my fig tree but my personal walk with Christ. It transformed my life, family and career. It was the beginning of starting my financial planning and investment practice, Fig Tree Wealth Management*.

*Fig Tree Wealth Management is a division of National Wealth Management LLC

Chapter 2

Even the Leaves

I chose this segment of the pruning process to be the first in this book because this was the beginning of my breakthrough and revelation. Now, before you start thinking that you made a mistake and started reading a book about gardening and pruning trees, let me say the following to keep you on track. "Even the Leaves" was the inspiration for the pruning of my finances and investments. I'll explain more in a bit. Let's go back to where I left off that late September with a fig tree full of un-ripened fruit and the looming possibility of losing the harvest to cold weather. My dreams of eating plump sweet figs, sharing them with family and friends, making fig jelly and putting figs on our salads, were now looking to be more of a nightmare. This was a major tease after all these years of putting in the work, seeing the fruit but just not being able to harvest them. I refused to give up and turned to the internet for help. I came across a video of a man showing his intel on how to get figs to ripen towards the end of the season. He said to take the leaves off the tree! Yes, the leaves. Not just the branches like most people think of when pruning. He said that removing the leaves allows more of the resources and nutrients to reach the fruit so they can ripen faster. "Wow", I thought to myself, "this is next level pruning". This made a lot of sense because I knew how big and tough fig leaves were. They have really thick stems full of sap and the leaves are also pretty thick, rugged and up to ten inches in height and width. This helps us understand how these became the first garments in history:

> "so they sewed fig leaves together
> and made coverings for themselves"
> Genesis 3:7

The solution still seemed too good to be true. So instead of committing to removing every leaf on the entire tree, I tested the theory out on just two branches. If, after removing the leaves from those two branches, I saw those figs ripen, then I'd move forward with removing the leaves from all the branches. So, I removed the leaves from two of the branches, which was about ten leaves per branch. Ready for it? Drum roll...... Not even two days later, the figs on only those branches started to ripen! They actually ripened and all the years of struggle made them taste that much sweeter. So you can guess what I did next right? I stripped the leaves off of that entire tree faster than a tornado swarm of apocalyptic locusts. Sure enough, one week later we reaped the full harvest of that tree and it was glorious! That's when it hit me. It was the same season that I had just learned about biblically responsible investing.

Biblically responsible investing or BRI as it is referred to, seeks to remove--or prune--companies from investment portfolios that go against our values and morals. Pruning the leaves that were preventing the fruit from ripening on my fig tree was the next level pruning that my fig tree had to undergo, just like my investments. Not only did I not realize that my investments were going against my beliefs, but that there was a better way to do it. I realized that I wanted to please God with my investments as well and that I didn't want to contribute to the collapse of biblical values in America. I didn't care about what it was going to cost me. In Proverbs 16:8 it says,

> "Better a little with righteousness
> than much gain with injustice."

I also knew that if I put God first in anything, He would take care of me:

> "But seek first the kingdom of God and his
> righteousness, and all these things
> will be added to you"
> Matthew 6:33

Now my hope is that as I help bring this knowledge to my readers and it will plant a seed in their hearts to make a change. The day I learned about BRI was the day my eyes were opened to the importance of making sure everything in my life honored God. I was thankful for the lesson from God through my fig tree about next level pruning.

In my career of almost twenty years in the financial services industry, I had exposure to many facets such as accounting, strategy, investment sales, investment analysis, retirement plans and market research. It wasn't until my role as a consultant to financial advisors that I met a lovely and wise woman. Unbeknownst to me, she was a Christian author and had written a book titled, *I Found Jesus In the Stock Market*. When I reached out to her to schedule an appointment to share my ideas and products as a consultant, she shared with me the concept of BRI. That phone call truly convicted me because I always knew that my investments had exposure to certain things against my morals. It opened my eyes to the possibility of investing in a new way. She sent me a copy of her book. I devoured that book and I immediately set out to change my investments. Once I submerged myself in the research, I started to be inspired and felt God was painting a bigger picture. I felt like it was time to use my years of experience in finance to help others honor God with their finances. I also had a strong feeling that I had to start my own division and not just join another group. While preparing the business plan and trying to outline the investment process, the vision of my fig tree and the next level pruning hit me! Pruning investments for God's glory in order to start to bear fruit or to bear more fruit. This was it! My mind started flooding with ideas, inspiration, emotion and excitement. That was the beginning concept of Fig Tree Wealth Management.

So exciting right? "So what did you do next Daniel?", you may be asking. Well, I put the idea on ice. That's right. I put the idea in a freezer and locked the door. Remember when I mentioned earlier that I was frustrated for many years of not bearing fruit or seeing fruit not ripen? During my financial services career working for other corporations, I had many side businesses that just never worked out. They all started with similar fervor and excitement but ended up just being a loss of money and time that I could've spent with family and friends. I was a "wantrepreneur". I was tired of the emotional rollercoaster ride.

There were two big differences in this particular career change. This was the first business I felt I was being called to. The other was that now I had a wife, kids, house and many more responsibilities. Starting another business was now a much bigger risk. So, I put the business plan together and then did nothing but pray and think about it. I asked God to show me clearly that this was what I was supposed to do. I wasn't going to take one step into this journey until I knew it was a calling for me. I was done dreaming.

Many opportunities presented themselves to nudge me in the direction to start this business, but I still had a wall up. One Sunday, my pastor spoke about God's calling on people and he strongly said "You are going to dream dreams again." Those words were for me and they filled me with emotion. I opened up my heart to God's will and doors started opening. He truly paved a way for me in so many ways that it gives Him all the glory when I share the testimony with people. My hope is that this book inspires everyone that has stopped dreaming to start dreaming again. For everyone who seems to barely have fruit or always seem to be a step behind their breakthrough, to start looking at where to start pruning.

In the process we will have uncomfortable moments and it will uncover perhaps where money and things were truly taking up space in our hearts and minds that belonged to God.

Once I knew that I wanted my practice to be God-centered, I enrolled in the Kingdom Advisors program offered through the Ron Blue Institute. A foundational bible verse from the program is Psalm 24:1 which says:

"The earth is the LORD's, and everything in it, the world, and all who live in it."

It is foundational because once we realize that we don't own what we have, but are mere stewards, it releases our grip and dependence on things. It gives us peace when we have to prune our finances and other aspects of our lives because we know we are in His hands. We stop worrying and having anxiety when the well we draw water from dries up because we know He can bring forth water from anywhere. It will help bring a Godly balance to life and allow us to advance the Kingdom with joy and peace. This verse will come up often in this book. I also learned that there were over 2300 Bible verses on finances and stewardship. God really does care about how we steward what we've been given. We'll walk through how to apply many of those verses as well.

Before we dig into the details of biblically responsible investing, let's look at why we even need it. Why do we have to strip even the leaves of our tree? If the fig tree was where it belonged, you typically wouldn't have to worry about such meticulous pruning. The same applies to our investment landscape and cultural environment. From the beginning of the stock market to where we are today, our country's commitment to moral values and biblical principles have slowly deteriorated. We are exposed to a lot more companies creating products for or supporting things that violate biblical values. Investment vehicles have also become more layered and complex making it more of a challenge to know what companies one is investing in. It's not like the old days of simply buying stocks. Now we have 401ks, IRAs, annuities and complex insurance policies with underlying investments of all sorts. One mutual fund alone can invest in 20, 50, 200 or more stocks and a typical retirement plan can have dozens of mutual funds within them. You can also just look at one mega sized US company and even though you are buying that stock because you are familiar with their main consumer product or service, you may not know the other companies and subsidiaries they own, what legislation they are contributing to or supporting and even what other countries they are benefiting. You can see how it can be a lot harder to invest in a God-friendly way and how important it is to prune even the leaves.

"They are not of the world, just as I am not of the world."
John 17:6

"But our citizenship is in heaven"
Philippians 3:20

As believers in Jesus, we are not of this world. We are exposed to sinful things and we need to be diligent in our pruning. In the same way that my fig tree needed extra pruning because it wasn't where it belonged, we need that next level pruning in our investments. Even the leaves!

This knowledge hit me like a ton of bricks. I felt like such a hypocrite in the sense that all these years, my investments were contributing to the very things I would speak against. It hit me even harder knowing the millions of Christians that are probably investing the same way without knowing it. I knew I was being called to make a difference. I didn't want to bring it to light to shame people, I wanted to offer them an alternative. There are many challenges to creating God-friendly investments, but after a few years I was thrilled to have created ones that were effective.

"Does God really care about our investment details? "Can't I just pretend I didn't hear about this and continue serving God in every other way?" "My investments returns may not come from the best sources but I give to church and charities from that money and turn it into a blessing". These where all questions and concerns that I also set out to answer in my research. What did the Bible say about such things?

"You must not bring the earnings of a female prostitute
or of a male prostitute into the house of
the LORD your God to pay any vow,
because the LORD your God detests them both."
Deuteronomy 23:18

Although this verse is specific to prostitution, it does show God's heart in the matter of not tithing or paying a vow with detestable monies. If we are profiting from investments in companies that are making or supporting things like abortion or pornography, we can't offer those earnings to God. "Well, what if I just shrug this away and not make a change?"

"Be doers of the word,
and not hearers only, deceiving yourselves."
James 1:22

Did you know that the pruning process does not only involve cutting away dead branches? You have to cut away living branches as well so that the best fruit can come forth and you can bear more of it. This was also true of all the leaves I pulled off my tree that were alive, but removing them allowed the fruit to ripen. Applied to your investing, this requires pruning companies from your portfolios that may have given you profits over the years and were alive. Pruning the living branches and leaves is difficult but you have to keep your focus on the righteous fruit you will bear for the Kingdom.

After reading this you may be saying, "Great, thanks Daniel for sharing this knowledge, now I feel guilty". Like I said earlier, I not only wanted people to hear the Word, but offer them an alternative so that they can be doers as well. People normally fear making a change, but I am here to help people understand and make the transition easy to digest. Remind yourself of Psalm 24:1 and that God owns it all. Release your grip knowing that it belongs to God and allow Him to bring about fruit in your life, whether it's financially or spiritually.

"Does this mean I can't drink coffee from this place or I can't buy clothes from that place?" It's important to draw the line somewhere. I believe that line is between consumption and profiting. When you buy a mutual fund or stock, you own a percentage of the underlying companies and you are therefore profiting from those companies. It's hard to see the link these days because everything is done electronically. In the past, an investor was issued a stock certificate for the shares bought. It looked similar to the title to a vehicle and was a symbol of one's ownership in the company and stake in the profits. If you merely consume a product, you aren't profiting from that company. If we really tried to avoid all of those companies for daily consumption purposes, we would probably not have many options left. It would also take up a lot of your time and freedom in your relationship with God in order to always be on top of that. Now don't get me wrong. I think it's wise to be an informed consumer and not only avoid the offensive companies but also reward good companies when we become aware of them. But investing is where we should take a strong stand.

The added benefit of biblically responsible investing is not only for our own faith convictions but because it can make a powerful impact and statement in this society. The size of the Christian investment market in the United States is estimated at over $21 trillion*. Imagine if we unified as believers and all made a shift to invest with our biblical values. It would rattle Wall Street

*Source: [Inspire Investing]
https://www.inspireinvesting.com/2019/05/01/biblically-responsible-investing-movement-exploding/

and corporate America! Did you know that Hilton Hotels stopped offering adult films on-demand in their hotel rooms in 2016? Were you aware that Chevron ended their abortion philanthropy in 2015? These major corporations will hear us when it starts to affect their bottom line. We need to stop saying that we are living in the end times and that there is nothing we can do about the moral decay in this country. If we are putting in the prayer for our nation and also doing our part, yet still see things getting worse, then we can chalk it up to end times. We need to be salt and light in this world.

"You are the salt of the earth. But if the salt loses its saltiness, how can it be made salty again? It is no longer good for anything, except to be thrown out and trampled underfoot. You are the light of the world. A town built on a hill cannot be hidden. Neither do people light a lamp and put it under a bowl. Instead they put it on its stand, and it gives light to everyone in the house. In the same way, let your light shine before others, that they may see your good deeds and glorify your Father in heaven."
Matthew 5:13-16

Portfolio managers and advisors focused on BRI face greater challenges in building diversified portfolios as they are omitting certain companies in industries like tobacco, which tend to do well in certain market environments. Although experienced and knowledgeable investment managers have been successful in navigating these performance challenges, it's important to let another Bible verse be our guide.

"Better a little with righteousness than much gain with injustice."
Proverbs 16:8

Sometimes when I share this concept with people and they ask, "How about XYZ Stock? Does that pass your screens?" Typically, it's a large well-known company that fails our screens and it's a company that they have made money with for years. Their body language changes as they realize they may have to prune what seems to be a living and fruitful branch. Some folks aren't willing to surrender those profits. It can be a similar experience to the young rich man in Mark 10:21 that asks what he needs to do in order to inherit eternal life. Jesus said to him "There is still one thing you haven't done. Go and sell all your possessions and give the money to the poor, and you will have treasure in heaven. Then come, follow me." The rich man walked away sad. Even though he said he had been following all the commandments throughout his life, he wasn't willing to obey Jesus with his riches. The same way some of the folks I talk to feel like they do everything else right, but aren't willing to align their investments with the Word. Even if we have to give up some performance or gain by investing in BRI, we need to have comfort in that we are acting in righteousness and that God will take care of us. However, the good news and the win-win is that you may not have to sacrifice performance to align your investments with your values. The Biblically Responsible Investing Institute conducted a comparison of the S&P 500 Index performance over the past twenty years versus a BRI screened portfolio. The results were promising in that while the BRI screened portfolio performed better in some periods and less favorably in others, it matched the return of the S&P 500 in the long run.*   Although we should be willing to sacrifice performance to invest with our values, historically speaking, we didn't have to as shown in their study.

Let's go deeper into how BRI portfolios are created. A common misconception is that we can only invest in Christian mutual funds or Christian companies. Although there are some great faith-centered funds and companies that we invest in, it's not the core of what our clients are invested in. We take the entire universe of stocks, bonds and mutual funds and run them through software which applies specific screens or filters. Those

*Source: [Screening the S&P 500 for Christian Values]
https://www.briinstitute.com/backtest.pdf

screens filter out things like abortion, pornography, tobacco, anti-family entertainment and more. We then look to understand why those investments are failing for those particular categories. For instance, if a stock is flagged for abortion, we look to see why they are failing for abortion. A company can fail the screening process if they are creating products or medicine to help facilitate abortions, or if they are heavy contributors and influencers helping to promote pro-abortion legislation. Major online retailers can be known for *distributing* adult content, but some may also be *creating* content for that industry. There are obvious companies like in the tobacco industry that you would assume would fail our screens but there are many companies that would surprise you. The bigger the company gets, the more they expand into different subsidiaries that are involved in all kinds of industries. There are also some companies that stick to their core product or services as they grow but are voracious contributors and core supporters of organizations violating biblical values. These are the leaves that we are pruning. It's also extremely important to monitor these investments on a regular basis to make sure they haven't changed in a matter to fail our criteria. We also utilize third-party research on companies in addition to keeping an eye on headlines for any changes or violations.

I have a strong passion for this investment process and love sharing it with others. I provide my clients not only with the information they need to understand the process, but also provide access to God-friendly portfolios. It has been rewarding to see the relief our clients have in that we've done the work to remove the leaves from their portfolios The same way that removing the leaves off my fig tree allowed the fruit to ripen, pruning my personal investments has opened the door for more Godly fruit. It inspired me to look at other areas of my finances that I could prune for God's glory.

Chapter 3

Pruning Our Finances

Our checkbooks and calendars reflect our priorities at the intersection of faith and works. The late Billy Graham once said, "Give me five minutes with a person's checkbook, and I will tell you where their heart is." Think about it for a second. If you took a look at what you spent your money on last year, what would it say about your priorities and disciplines? If you looked at your calendar last year and saw what you spent your time on, what would it say about your faith and focus? Some of my clients are afraid of the following word and actually refer to it as the "B" word. I'm gonna say it, so cover your ears (but not your eyes). *Budget.* Some people feel that a budget takes away their freedom and enjoyment of life. What they are really afraid of is what putting together a budget will bring to light. It's hard to swallow when you find out how much you are overspending. I'm going to cover how a budget doesn't have to be enslaving but how it can set you free. If it makes you feel better, let's call it *expense planning*.

Before we get into the mechanics of expense planning, let's go back to our foundational verse:

"The earth is the LORD's, and everything in it, the world, and all who live in it."
Psalm 24:1

If we remind ourselves that God owns everything and that we are mere stewards of what He has given us, it starts to open our hearts to the planning. You have to ask yourself where all your money is going.   Let's start with this exercise. Take a look at the list below of the different ways that we can spend money and think about how much you spent on each last year. Write in a percentage for each of the categories on the next page:

Current Spending Allocation

Living Expenses/Family Provision:

Debt:

Taxes:

Saving:

Investing:

Tithe:

Charity:

This exercise alone may start opening your eyes to where you need to start pruning. Perhaps you are now overwhelmed and are staring at a big tree that needs a lot of pruning. Perhaps you don't know where to start. Let's work our way backwards and start with 0% in each category and after we look at a biblical perspective, you can fill in the categories again with your goal.

The biggest piece of the pie for most in America is the living and consumption bucket. Our society is trained to believe that the more stuff we have, the happier we will be. We can't turn on the television without being bombarded with shows boasting materialism and all the commercials sprinkled in between that basically say, "buy this product, you need this product right now, it will make you happier." Message after message that we need a more expensive car… we need new clothes…we need another vacation… spoil yourself… your family won't be happy unless… house is too small…we need to make more … and we need to borrow more. We don't even need to open the Bible to know that having more stuff doesn't equal more happiness. Often times it's the opposite. The extra "stuff" can start to cloud our view of what really matters and it adds to the stress and anxiety in our lives. So, what is missing? Contentment.

Perhaps you have said or heard others saying, "I wish I had a bigger house, we are running out of space," only to move into a bigger house and then say, "If I only had one more room in the house, I could have an arcade room". Or they wish they could have a nicer car, and after getting one, they say, "I wish I had heated seats". If I were to ask you, "how much money do you need to be rich?". Some people might say $1 million. Others might say $10 million. I like to watch people try to think of a number as they typically start with one amount and then add a few more as they start imagining extra houses or additional things to buy. If we suddenly received a million dollars, how quickly would we turn around and say that we need more. There is nothing wrong with wanting more blessings for our lives as many of us know the prayer of Jabez:

"Oh, that you would bless me and enlarge my territory"
1 Chronicles 4:10

That carries over into the new testament as well:

"God is able to bless you abundantly, so that in all things at all times, having all that you need, you will abound in every good work."
2 Corinthians 9:8

The problem lies in not being content in the current situation while waiting for God to enlarge our territory. I also believe firmly that God wants us to enjoy our lives and the things He has blessed us with. Contentment gives us the ability to enjoy life.

"Moreover, when God gives someone wealth and possessions, and the ability to enjoy them, to accept their lot and be happy in their toil—this is a gift of God."
Ecclesiastes 5:19

So let's dive in to understand what contentment is. Dictionaries define the word as "a state of satisfaction". I also think the word "thankful" should be added to the definition. I believe that thankfulness and contentment go hand in hand. Let's do a quick exercise. Pause for one minute and think about your life. Are you content? Are you thankful for your current situation? Maybe your situation isn't the rosiest and you think that it's not possible to be content. What does the Bible say about the matter? Here is a powerful verse that the Apostle Paul wrote while in a Roman prison:

"Not that I speak from want, for I have learned to be content in whatever circumstances I am. I know how to get along with humble means, and I also know how to live in prosperity; in any and every circumstance I have learned the secret of being filled and going hungry, both

of having abundance and suffering need. I can do all
things through Him who strengthens me."
Philippians 4:11-13

How would you feel if you were sitting in a jail for
preaching the Gospel? Is sitting in jail better than your
current situation? So how is it possible to be content
while in jail? It has everything to do with Paul knowing
that he was in jail for Christ and that his reward was in
Heaven. He was thankful and satisfied knowing that God
had a bigger plan. Paul also knew how to be content in
prosperity.

Compared to the rest of the world, especially in
third world countries, even lower income Americans are
comparatively "rich". So why aren't we truly happy and
satisfied with our lives? The further we move away from
a biblical foundation and away from a relationship with
God, the emptier we feel and the more we acquire stuff to
fill the void. Television and social media throw gasoline
on the fire of us wanting the things that wealthy people
flaunt. Here is another powerful verse:

"But godliness with contentment is great gain. For we
brought nothing into the world, and we can take nothing
out of it. But if we have food and clothing, we will be
content with that. People who want to get rich fall into
temptation and a trap and into many foolish and harmful

31

desires that plunge men into ruin and destruction. For the love of money is a root of all kinds of evil. Some people, eager for money, have wandered from the faith and pierced themselves with many griefs."
1 Timothy 6:6-12

Let's dissect that verse a bit. The desire to get rich is compared to falling into a trap. While reading that verse, I got a vision of someone falling into a large hole in the ground and trying to claw their way up the muddy sides to get out. No matter how hard they tried, they never reached the top because the top was never defined. In our lives, we can grind, grind and grind but never reach a point of freedom or satisfaction. I often hear one of those verses used incorrectly by saying that money is the root of all evil. The Bible says it's the *love* of money, not just money itself. Money in the hands of the foolish can be destructive, but money in the hands of a content and generous person can produce righteous fruit. Now that we have an understanding of contentment, we are getting closer to tackling how to allocate our money towards living expenses. Our next step will be to look at debt and taxes. We all know what happens when you don't pay your taxes and many of us know what Jesus said when asked about taxes.

"Give back to Caesar what is Caesar's and to God what is God's."
Mark 12:17

If we put aside the negative images of greedy tax collectors and negative references to the government as "the man", taxes can do a lot of good in our society. That money contributes to funding roads, schools, defense and other programs. What if we stopped looking at taxes as a curse, but instead as a reflection of God's provision in our lives. Generally, if we are paying more in taxes, it means that God has provided us an increase in income or earnings. However, the tax code does allow for us to minimize our tax bill by allocating assets towards charities or gifting to others. Tax planning is an important part of our process. It allows us to discover ways to minimize the "tax bite", while allowing our clients to achieve various goals such as: contributing to a loved one's college savings plan, giving more money to their church or favorite non-profits and also donating appreciated assets like stocks or real estate. In certain cases, it makes more sense to donate $10,000 worth of stock than it is to cut a check from your bank account. Why is that? Let's say you bought those stock shares for $5,000 total and it increased to $10,000, if you went to sell that stock in order to donate the money, you would have to pay capital gains tax first on the $5,000. So now your contribution would be $10,000 minus the tax you paid. Instead, you can donate the stock outright to the charity, and they are in charge of selling the stock. You avoid the tax bite and you now have the ability to deduct your contribution. As financial planners, we are often the quarterbacks for a client in regards to working with their accountant, estate attorney and other professionals. It's always important to consult with a tax professional to assist in charitable giving and tax planning. Once someone has amassed a sizeable estate, tax planning can be crucial for making sure they aren't paying excessive taxes and that the estate is passing on strategically to loved ones and/or charities. We have heard of horror stories of massive estates that had to be liquidated and most of the estate went towards taxes instead of the remaining family members and/or charities. It's important to give for the desire to bless others and not merely to save on taxes. This is like letting the tail wag the dog.

"But love your enemies, and do good, and lend, expecting nothing in return, and your reward will be great, and you will be sons of the Most High, for he is kind to the ungrateful and the evil."
Luke 6:35

What separates us from how the rest of the world gives, including the ultra-wealthy, is that we should give without expecting anything in return. We should give to bless others and expand the Kingdom. To save on taxes is an added benefit of giving. So when it comes to taxes, the government dictates how much that piece of the pie will be and we can use wisdom to make sure it isn't a bigger slice than it should be.

Unlike taxes, debt is a piece of the pie that we have full control of. It's your choice whether you are going to borrow money to purchase something today or save up and buy it when you have enough. I don't believe that all borrowing is troublesome especially when there is low interest on the loan. If you can be disciplined enough to save up for a house and pay cash for it, go for it, but it's very difficult, especially in certain areas of the country. I want to focus more on consumer debt in this book. A credit card in the hands of a wise steward will allow them to earn cash or reward points while paying off the full balance every month. A credit card in the hands of a compulsive over spender can result in anxiety, depression, bankruptcy and even divorce. There is an old saying that says "If you want to lose a friend, loan him money". There are many verses and warnings in the Bible about debt.

"The rich rules over the poor, and the borrower is the slave of the lender." Proverbs 22:7

"Let no debt remain outstanding except the continuing debt to love on another." Romans 13:8

"The wicked borrows and does not repay, But the righteous shows mercy and gives." Psalm 37:21

What does the world tell you? Satisfy your craving today for things you can't afford by borrowing. Remember the credit card commercial that said "don't leave home without it?" Now they changed it to "don't live life without it." The Word tells us to avoid debt; the world tells us to not live life without it. God wants you to live free and credit card companies want to make money off of your interest payments. I have worked with many clients that had balances carrying over every month on 3 to 6 credit cards and only being able to afford the minimum payments, in addition to student loans with high interest rates. The Bible uses slavery as a comparison. As a financial professional, I have seen the oppression, shame, anger, frustration, anxiety, fear and division that debt can cause. Borrowers feel trapped and don't see a way out of their situation. It's important to stop the spending and reach out to a financial professional for help. Excessive debt and overspending can often be indicators of a spiritual issue and lack of balance. It's the outward manifestation of trying to fill a void that only God can. Seeking God through prayer and reading the Word, as well as finding Godly counsel is the way to start. I am a big fan of debt snowball programs made popular by Dave Ramsey. Most people try to pay off the highest interest credit cards first but the debt snowball program starts by paying off the lowest balance first. Once the first card is paid off, all of the extra goes towards the second card, and so on. Getting out of debt is often a battle of the mind, and this system helps people feel good about the process psychologically by getting quick wins. It's so rewarding to see people pay off their first credit card and get inspired to continue the process. They start to taste the freedom as they see the first chain fall off and have a greater chance of sticking to the plan. I encourage all of my clients to pray for the things they need and can't afford. Allow God to bless you, to open doors and to give you wisdom on the particular need. Allow God to step in as your provider and replace your dependence on debt.

The Bible also speaks to investing and saving. What would happen if you reaped the harvest of a field you planted and consumed all of the crop without planting seed for the future? Hunger would be in your near future unless of course someone gave you some of their crops. The same happens to folks today that live only for the moment and forget to save for the future. This can also happen with good intentions towards others. A common example involves parents spending every penny they have on their home and providing materially fulfilling lives for their children and putting them through the most expensive colleges, only to later in life find themselves a few years away from retirement with a shortfall in their retirement funds. Now, the adult children have to fill the income gap and help support their parents in their retirement years. While well-intended, this is a common scenario of a lack of balance in spending and investing and a major problem in America for retirees facing income gaps due to underfunded retirement plans. Often, this is a result of not saving enough, not taking enough risk in the earlier years or taking too much risk when nearing retirement. The fear and lack of understanding in how to assess risk causes the "put cash under the mattress" syndrome. Let's read what the Bible says about this syndrome:

> "Again, it will be like a man going on a
> journey, who called his servants and
> entrusted his wealth to them. To one he
> gave five bags of gold, to another two bags,
> and to another one bag, each according to
> his ability. Then he went on his journey. The
> man who had received five bags of gold
> went at once and put his money to work and

gained five bags more. So also, the one with two bags of gold gained two more. But the man who had received one bag went off, dug a hole in the ground and hid his master's money. After a long time the master of those servants returned and settled accounts with them. The man who had received five bags of gold brought the other five. 'Master,' he said, 'you entrusted me with five bags of gold. See, I have gained five more.' His master replied, 'Well done, good and faithful servant! You have been faithful with a few things; I will put you in charge of many things. Come and share your master's happiness!'

The man with two bags of gold also came. 'Master,' he said, 'you entrusted me with two bags of gold; see, I have gained two more.' "His master replied, 'Well done, good and faithful servant! You have been faithful with a few things; I will put you in charge of many things. Come and share your master's happiness!' Then the man who had received one bag of gold came. 'Master,' he said, 'I knew that you are a hard man, harvesting where you have not sown and gathering where you have not scattered seed.

So I was afraid and went out and hid your gold in the ground. See, here is what belongs to you.' His master replied, 'You wicked, lazy servant! So you knew that I harvest where I have not sown and gather where I have not scattered seed? Well then, you should have put my money on deposit with the bankers, so that when I returned I would have received it back with interest. So take the bag of gold from him and give it to the one who has ten bags. For whoever has will be given more, and they will have an abundance. Whoever does not have, even what they have will be taken from them"
Matthew 25:14-30

Although Jesus was teaching about talents and not finances per se in this parable, it still shows an important financial principle. He highlights the importance and the power of interest. Compounding interest, for example, happens when you are promised interest by a bank in your savings account. As you reinvest that interest, your principal grows by the interest amount of a higher balance and you earn interest off of that higher balance when it's paid out the next time. In the context of investing, the power of compounding returns can help money grow faster and outpace inflation, with interest as well as through capital appreciation from the market. Putting money under the mattress will keep you from spending it but it's purchasing power decreases as things get more expensive over time. You not only want to make sure you keep pace with inflation but you also want to grow your money above inflation if your risk tolerance and time horizon allows it. Investing is an important part of attaining future goals and plans.

"For which of you, desiring to build a tower, does not first sit down and count the cost, whether he has enough to complete it?"
Luke 14:28

Counting the cost of your goals and knowing the time frame of when you want to achieve them will allow you to choose the right investments and the right amount of risk to take. As you keep adding more money throughout the months and years, compounding returns can be the wind at your back to help you achieve those goals.

The final way in which we can spend money is by giving. I saved this bucket for last because this will actually be the first piece of the pie we will start with when pruning and making any changes. After we walk through what the Word says about giving, it will make a lot more sense as to why we should start with our giving goal and then adjust our life and other expenditures around that. Let's read what the scripture says about giving to God and others.

"A generous person will prosper; whoever refreshes others will be refreshed."
Proverbs 11:25

This verse uses a word that many Christians are afraid to use these days and that is "prosperity". Certain televangelists and prosperity preachers have tarnished this word. It has even created uncomfortableness for pastors to mention from the pulpit about being obedient to tithing or giving offerings during a service at the risk of being labeled "money hungry". Prosperity is deeper than just having money and material things. You can have ten million dollars in the bank and not have prosperity. Biblical prosperity starts when someone is spiritually rich through becoming less, so that God can become greater in them. A generous person that refreshes others as described in this proverb will prosper because they already have a heart free from the love of money. When we give to Jesus our fish and loaves, He multiplies it to bless the multitudes and in turn we have plenty to eat as well. Once we understand the miracle of giving, we become conduits and pipelines of blessings to others while God supplies our needs.

"You will be enriched in every way so that you can be generous on every occasion, and through us your generosity will result in thanksgiving to God."
2 Corinthians 9:11

God will give us more when we are generous so that we can in turn give more. We don't give to get, but when our hearts give freely and cheerfully, we are blessed in return.

"Give, and it will be given to you. A good measure, pressed down, shaken together and running over, will be poured into your lap. For with the measure you use, it will be measured to you."
Luke 6:38

This is where true prosperity lies with a foundation in contentment. This is why the title of this book is *Prune & Prosper*. Biblical prosperity is the goal.

Now let's discuss the tithe to God. This should be the very first thing we budget for in our expense plan. Here are two commonly used verses that speak to tithing:

"Honor the Lord with your wealth, with the firstfruits of all your crops."
Proverbs 3:9

"Bring the whole tithe into the storehouse, that there may be food in my house. Test me in this," says the Lord Almighty, "and see if I will not throw open the floodgates of heaven and pour out so much blessing that there will not be room enough to store it."
Malachi 3:10

Many biblically based financial teachers have pointed to the fact that this is the only place in the Bible where God says to test Him and see. Why is that? God knows that we often put our trust in money and material things. Allocating a portion of our earnings back to God, releases that trust back to Him and displays not only our faith but also our thankfulness. I've had clients say to me, "We've been tithing for years but we've never seen the abundance that the Bible mentions." After dissecting their situation, we were able to uncover various reasons why. We can't just be faithful in putting gasoline in our car but neglect changing the oil or the tires and expect the car to run as expected. In the same manner, it's important to follow all of the biblical principles. For some of my clients, they were giving in order to get something in return or giving out of obligation. God wants us to give cheerfully and without reluctance.

"Whoever sows sparingly will also reap sparingly, and whoever sows generously will also reap generously.

Each of you should give what you have decided in your heart to give, not reluctantly or under compulsion, for God loves a cheerful giver."
2 Corinthians 9:6-7

In some cases, they were giving generously but also accumulating debt. They were investing and getting the same return or significantly lower than what they were paying back to the credit card companies in interest. In many cases, they were tithing but allocating way too much to consumption and accumulating "stuff", and not saving for a rainy day or investing in order to achieve future goals. We have to be honest with ourselves and identify what is causing the weeds and thorns to grow in our lives and choking out our ability to thrive. It is vital to align our finances with all of the biblical principles in order to reap the harvest that God promises. It's even more important to allow God to teach us contentment and to also keep our awareness of spiritual blessings we have received instead of just financial. I've worked with many clients of different walks and it's awesome to see the blessings of God and His faithfulness when someone commits to being a good steward, not only in giving, but in every aspect of their lives. It empowers them.

If we only have a near-term perspective in our giving, we miss out on the big picture. When we have an eternal perspective, it allows us to stop worrying about today and shifts our actions to invest in the Kingdom.

"Do not store up for yourselves treasures on earth, where moths and vermin destroy, and where thieves break in and steal. But store up for yourselves treasures in heaven, where moths and vermin do not destroy, and where thieves do not break in and steal. For where your treasure is, there your heart will be also."
Mathew 6:19-21

Verse after verse in the Bible points to the power and blessing of giving. The blessings go beyond this world and are more important than anything material. I always wondered how my giving would change if I got an actual glimpse of Heaven. How do you think your giving would change if you got a brief tour of Heaven and a preview of your potential eternal treasures? I think that the stresses of our present situations would lose their place in our minds and our desire to amass stuff in this world would be replaced with a focus on storing up treasures in Heaven.

So now that we've covered the various ways that we can spend money and what the Bible says about each of them, let's rebuild our priorities to how we want to start spending money today. Take a few minutes to pray right now and ask God how He would have you allocate money and prune your expenses. Ask for wisdom in the whole process.

Welcome back! Now fill in the percentages on the next page starting with Tithing and end with Living.

New Spending Goal

Tithe:

Charity:

Saving:

Investing:

Debt:

Taxes:

Living Expenses/Family Provision:

Now that you have your new goal for spending based on our biblical discussion, it's time to prune any areas of the categories in order to shift resources around. In order to give more, you may have to pull from your living expenses. There may also be ways to reduce your tax liabilities in order to give more. Perhaps you need to pull from some of your savings to pay off high interest credit card debt in order to free up income for charitable giving. The majority of the time, it comes down to the expense planning we talked about earlier. The good ole' "B" word. The *budget*.

The reason people think it's a bad word is because they feel it will end their life of fun and luxury. They feel they will be tied down to it, like a ball and chain, every time a purchase needs to be made. Why are we more willing to hold on to loose spending which is robbing our joy and financial peace, and less willing to put everything down on a spreadsheet and work our way to freedom? "Well, wait a minute Daniel." "Did you say luxury?" "I don't have a mansion, yacht or private jet." In order to embark on pruning our spending, we need to make a distinction between *needs* and *wants*. Often times we confuse necessities with luxuries. Is it a necessity to spend $5 a day on coffee at your local shop when you could easily make it for $0.50 cents or less at home? That's over $1,600 yearly that could have been used to pay down debt, save, invest or give. The same concept can apply to eating out versus making meals at home or bringing lunch from home to work. How many times have we heard people criticizing a believer for driving an $80,000 car even though their annual salary is $1,000,000 or more, which is 8% of their salary, yet we often see people with an annual salary of $100,000 or less and driving a $36,000 SUV which is 36% of their salary. These are one of the most common luxury items that people feel like they *need* and will use loans and expensive lease contracts to attain them now. If you are struggling to make ends meet or never have enough surplus to invest for your future or give, it's important to start looking at which luxuries are draining your finances. I still think it is important to enjoy some of these things in life, but doing so with balance and planning is crucial. Many times, when I am helping a married couple prune their budget in order to get out of debt, eating out and entertainment tend to be excessive expenditures. I always encourage them to continue doing their date nights and enjoying activities together but with less costly alternatives. You can still have a date night over pizza and salad instead of a multi-course meal at a gourmet restaurant. Taking walks together is not only free, but there are studies that show the overall benefits for a healthy marriage. It doesn't take a lot of effort to search the internet for fun and free activities in your area. The greatest memories I have with my children and memories that they often bring up, are when we were fishing, exploring for colorful rocks in a river, lemonade stands, making forts and paper airplanes and low-cost day trips. You don't have to sacrifice fun and quality time in order to prune your budget. You just have to get creative and put in the time.

Once you have a strong grasp on distinguishing between your *needs* and *wants*, create a spreadsheet or a simple written list of your current monthly expenses broken out by fixed and variable costs. Fixed costs will be your rent, water and electric bills, etc. Variable expenses will include things like clothing, entertainment, dining out, etc. See the example on the next page:

Monthly Budget

Income	Variable Expenses
Net salary:	Food/Household items:
Investments:	Clothes:
Rental:	Dining out:
Other:	Entertainment:
Total Income:	Gas/Auto maintenance:
	Vacation:
Fixed Expenses	Medical/Dental:
	Cell phone:
Tuition/Fees/Supplies:	Cable/Internet:
Rent/Mortgage:	Gifts:
Utilities:	Personal care:
Home Phone:	Charity:
Credit Card/Loans:	Other:
Insurance (home/vehicle/health):	**Total Variable Expenses:**
Vehicle Registration:	Plus+
Tithe:	**Total Fixed Expenses:**
Other:	**=Total Monthly Expenses:**
Total Fixed Expenses:	**Total Income:**
	Minus -
	Total Expenses:
	=Surplus or Deficit:

When your list is complete, you can take a step back and really see where all your money has been going. It's the same way I used to take step back from my fig tree to take a good look at the entire tree before pruning. Your list of expenses allows you to see which branches you need to prune in order to free up resources to pay down debt, save, invest and give. Some folks are disciplined enough to remember this list and stick to it. Other folks that struggle in this area and are prone to over spending with credit cards should develop a cash bucket or envelope system. This works by setting aside cash on a monthly basis and earmarking each envelope for those variable categories such as clothing, dining out, entertainment, etc. As soon as your paycheck hits your bank account, you take the cash out of the bank and use it to spend on what you have pre-determined. That way, if in a certain month you deplete your clothing budget early in the month, you will have to take money out of the entertainment or other bucket if you want to buy that extra piece of clothing. It helps to create a strong spending discipline and crucial will power to not always give in to any craving. This doesn't mean you have to live with this system for the rest of your life, but it's a great way to set you on the path towards an increase in your spending awareness. I remember reading a book by Larry Burkett in my early twenties which taught me about the same envelope system. It helped me to stop adding to the credit card debt

I had and, although I used the system for only one year, I carried the discipline and awareness with me through the years. You will be amazed at the strength you develop to not give in to impulse buying for stuff you think you need in the moment. Even if you have a weak moment and buy something you shouldn't have, you know that you have taken away from another one of your spending categories for that month. In the moments that you are able to resist, you are rewarded with knowing that you are staying on track with hitting your goals of giving, saving and investing.

Many people today struggle with their finances because of lack of knowledge and education in this area. In school, we are not taught how to manage our finances and especially not in the area of biblical stewardship. But, once we have the knowledge and put it into practice, we need to teach this to our children, grandchildren, nieces and nephews and other children that we mentor. Proverbs 22:6 can also apply to financial stewardship when it says, "Start children off on the way they should go, and even when they are old they will not turn from it." One of the fun exercises you can do with children is to create envelopes or jars each labeled with "God", "Charity", "Me" and "Savings/Investing". On each jar or envelope, write out Bible verses on each type of spending (like the ones I used for each category in this book). You can also discuss the option of debt in the sense that they can borrow money from you but they will have to pay it back with interest. Walk them through each type of spending category and what the Bible says for each one. They should start grasping the importance of giving back to God, giving to those in need and saving for their future. Once you feel they have a good understanding, give them $10 in singles or another amount that's easy enough to divide up and still be meaningful for each category. Ask them to divide up the money into each envelope or jar based on the biblical view you shared with them. Don't forget; they are children and they might just put all the money in the "Me" jar because they've been wanting a toy that costs exactly $10. It's ok for them to put some in this category. Don't make them feel bad or shame them for their choice. Take that opportunity to explain the importance of each category again and the impact they could have by giving to a charity that helps children that don't have toys or even food. Teach them to trust in God to be their provider despite their own desires. It's such a joy to watch children grasp a biblical perspective to their money and the heart they begin to develop to help others.

Chapter 4

Pruning Our Time

Pruning how we spend time is just as important as how we spend our money. Billy Graham's quote about knowing someone by their checkbook, can also apply to knowing someone's priorities and faith by looking at their calendar. What we spend our time on reflects where our heart is. In the same way that our financial budgets can reveal how spending may not align with our beliefs, analyzing how we spend our time can reveal some surprises as well. Many of us have the desire to put God first in our lives, but our time allocation may not reflect that. What I often find is that we are out of balance. It's easy to spend way too much time on some things and not enough time on others. This lack of balance can bring with it symptoms like anxiety, fear, emptiness, burn-out, stress and strife. So before we dig in to what the Bible says about how we should spend our time, take a moment to reflect on how you spent your time last year, last month, last week and yesterday. Now try to average it out to a typical week and estimate the percentage of time you spent on the following categories on the next page:

Current Time Allocation

Work/School:

Social Media/Smartphones:

Family & Friends:

Exercise:

Rest:

Practice on Talent:

Hobbies:

Prayer:

Reading Bible:

Church:

Ministry/Volunteer/Charity:

Now take a moment to step back and look at your categories as you would a tree that needs pruning. What areas have produced fruit in your life and what areas have hindered your fruitfulness? What category can you prune to make time for a more effective one? Are you seeing a healthy biblical balance to your time allocation?

"Look carefully then how you walk, not as unwise but as wise, making the best use of the time, because the days are evil. Therefore do not be foolish, but understand what the will of the Lord is."
Ephesians 5:15-17

Let's take a look at what the Word says for some of the categories.

Work and school are typically where people spend most of their time. The biggest issue I see in America and in the church is that we are working too much. I'll tackle this in a bit. Josiah Gilbert Holland is credited with the saying, "God gives every bird it's food, but does not throw it into the nest." This quote speaks to the obvious point that we need to work, but it also illustrates the importance of not just waiting at home for a blessing to arrive. It also reminds us that God is the ultimate provider and that we don't have to worry about our needs and where they will come from. We just have to go out there and get it. We have to sow the seeds that

God provides. Although most of the readers of this book probably have a strong work ethic, the Bible does speak often about the importance of being diligent in our work and to avoid laziness. Below are some examples:

"All hard work brings a profit, but mere talk leads only to poverty."
Proverbs 14:23

This verse can apply to some people that only talk about how hard they work or want to work, but then don't. It does speak to a lot of us that have a great product idea, a special talent, a strong business idea, a powerful concept for a book, or a calling for ministry, only to just talk about it with no action. You know you should be pursuing something yet you keep putting it off year after year and forgoing a potential opportunity to grow wealth and bless others.

"A little sleep, a little slumber, a little folding of the hands to rest—
and poverty will come on you like a thief and scarcity like an armed man."
Proverbs 6:10-11

Many folks that are living pay check to pay check sometimes don't even realize how close they are to financial hardship and even poverty. It's important to evaluate whether it's an issue of living beyond your means or that you may need to work more or change career paths to increase your income.

"Anyone who does not provide for their relatives, and especially for their own household, has denied the faith and is worse than an unbeliever."
1 Timothy 5:8

This verse reaffirms that our love and faith must be put into action. It's a biblical responsibility to work in order to provide for our families.

Now let's take a look at another verse that provides a different perspective:

"Those who work their land will have abundant food, but those who chase fantasies have no sense."
Proverbs 12:11

This last verse about chasing fantasies reminds me of a few things I've heard from people and have seen on social media. Playing the lottery is one of the ways that I see folks putting time and money into the wrong place and chasing fantasies. "Imagine if I won $100 million dollars! I would buy this, do that, donate this much." The Bible says in Proverbs 13:11: "Wealth gained hastily will dwindle, but whoever gathers little by little will increase it." Another way to say it is, "easy come, easy go". I've come across social media pages from people embracing fantasies of being rich, being an entrepreneur and "faking it until they make it". The "About Me" sections on their pages say that they are self-employed and CEOs of ten different "companies" that they "run". Meanwhile they are just random hustles and mild schemes. Most of their pictures are of themselves wearing fancy clothes (that I hope they can afford), and of themselves next to really expensive cars that they've probably come across in parking lots and don't actually own. They are just chasing fantasies. There is no substitute for working hard, working smart, filling a need and adding value. Putting in the work while you are young, will allow you to reap a harvest when you are old. Once your body is tired and may face potential health issues, it's a lot harder to work passionately. You also don't want to face the temptation of taking more risk in your investments at an older age in order to fill an income gap. I always encourage my clients to plan now for what they want to do in retirement and work towards achieving those goals.

It's not uncommon to come across people that aren't too thrilled with their job. This may be a life changing area that you feel called to prune. Don't just get stuck in a job. Pray for God to give you wisdom and to open doors while you seek other options. If you are meant to stay there for a season, ask God to give you peace while you are there and to give you opportunities to share the Gospel with co-workers and/or clients. Remember that even if you have a boss or manager to report to, God is who you really work for. This will help you to release your anxieties about your workplace and focus on working hard and smart while using your talents.

"Whatever you do, work at it with all your heart, as working for the Lord, not for human masters, since you know that you will receive an inheritance from the Lord as a reward. It is the Lord Christ you are serving."
Colossians 3:23-24

Corporate offices are riddled with employees that are constantly on their smartphones texting people and on social media while they are supposed to be working. Be equally diligent when your boss isn't around and no one is looking because you know that God is watching and waiting to bless you.

Remind yourself every day that your workplace can be a mission field. I can't tell you how many times I prayed for God to lead me to someone in need right before entering the workplace in the morning and an opportunity clearly presented itself. One time it happened as soon as I walked in and a co-worker that was forty years older than me asked if I would pray for him and his son who just got diagnosed with cancer. I added the fact that he was much older than me to also illustrate that with God's wisdom and favor, we can be relevant to anyone, anytime and anyplace. When we pray like that daily, it not only invites God to put people in our path but it also opens our eyes to opportunities that have been in front of our eyes for years. We stop thinking about how that person may annoy us or what they did to us and focus on blessing them with the help of grace. We stop judging the world and see them through the compassionate eyes of Jesus. Prune your view of work, how you work, who you really work for; you will then bear more fruit.

Let's go back to my prior comment on how we may be working too much. How often do we bump into people and when we ask how they are doing, they reply with, "I'm grinding". You can see the stress on their face and the lack of rest. Sometimes we overwork ourselves in our jobs and also say yes to every opportunity that presents itself at church. We enroll our kids in every sport and activity under the sun. We then have to drive them around the world to every practice and games that come with it. We work at work. We work at ministry. We work on our marriages. We work at being good parents. We work to better ourselves. It's no surprise that burn-out is so common not only in our personal lives, but also in the church. We can be so busy serving in our churches and ministries that we neglect to spend time with God who is the reason we are serving. Working hard at our jobs and serving are important, but there must be balance. There must be rest for the body and rest for the mind. This lack of balance is evident with how many Christians casually obey the commandment to keep the Sabbath.

"Remember the Sabbath day by keeping it holy. Six days you shall labor and do all your work, but the seventh day is a sabbath to the Lord your God. On it you shall not do any work, neither you, nor your son or daughter, nor your male or female servant, nor your animals, nor any foreigner residing in your towns. For in six days the Lord made the heavens and the earth, the sea, and all that is in them, but he rested on the seventh day. Therefore the Lord blessed the Sabbath day and made it holy."
Exodus 20:8-11

Unfortunately, our addiction to work in order to afford the lifestyles we have chosen, often leads to compromising the Sabbath. It becomes more important for people to use that seventh day to get some overtime or get that extra work in for more money. In the same way that you give God your tithe and trust He will take care of your needs, the same should apply to giving the Lord the Sabbath. Do you want to squeeze out a few extra dollars with anxiety and lack of peace, or do you want to put the Kingdom first and open the door for His blessings? If one of the top fast food chains in the country can honor God by being closed on Sunday and be successful, so can you! In my twenty years of being in the workforce and keeping the Sabbath holy, I've never been in want. There have been many instances where I was asked to work or was presented with a reason to compromise, but I never gave in. I always prayed for wisdom and asked God to help me out of any situation that would hurt my commitment to Him. He has always been faithful. We just have to decide to make it important to us. I understand that people have complicated and unique situations, but with God, all things are possible. Pray for wisdom and a way. I also know that many people have jobs that require them to work on the weekends and have a random day off during the week. Then I encourage you to make that day during the week your Sabbath. Take the day to rest and enjoy a day in fellowship with God, family and friends. Make sure you are also resting your mind. Tell the hamster running on the wheel in your brain to take the day off also. Ask God for His peace in your life so you can actually rest and prune away the thoughts and activities that could be giving you anxiety. It's time to prune your week to make sure you are balancing hard work with a blessed day that God carved out for you.

How many times have you heard or said the phrase, "I just don't have the time." Most often it really means, "I'm just not making the time for it." Pruning time in order to make time was vital for me to be able to write this book. Being married with three children and running my financial planning practice can pose a serious challenge to finding time to write and be inspired. I also didn't want to take time away from God in order to do it either. I started spending less time on social media throughout the day and used writing the book as filler time. If you are honest with yourself and how much time you allocate each day to social media, you will find a great opportunity to prune and use that time for something more fruitful. During my downtime at night (once the kids were asleep), I enjoyed playing a game on my tablet. The game was free, fun and helped take my mind off of work. After reflecting on my allocation of time, I had to temporarily prune some of this "play and unwind" time for the benefit of writing the book. I knew that this was an opportune time to write the book while the house was nice and quiet. It's amazing when you are looking for free time to accomplish something, you start becoming more aware of little ten minute to thirty-minute opportunities throughout your day. These are also great opportunities to seek God in prayer and read the Word.

The beauty of our relationship with God is that the lines of communication are always open and we can talk to Him throughout the day. We can thank Him briefly before eating a meal or quickly ask for guidance when we are about to start a task. We can also prune our words and behaviors as we go about our daily lives by repenting and asking for strength on the spot. However, it is vital for any believer to spend quiet and quality time with God in prayer. There is something special to carving out time to seek Him early in the morning. While the world is quiet, while your mind is still calm, and while your house is peaceful, God shows up in wonderful ways.

"But I, O Lord, cry to you; in the morning my prayer comes before you."
Psalm 88:13

In the same way we give the Lord our first fruits, it shows God how important He is to us when we give him the first of the day. It can be hard to do, but so worth the effort. It helps our day start out right, balanced and with the right mind set. I also believe that ending our day in prayer before going to sleep and squeezing some alone time in the middle of the day, helps us keep our fire lit and our mind on the Kingdom. If you are going to prune other areas in your life to make time, prayer and reading the Word should get first dibs on that extra time.

"You will seek me and find me, when you seek me with
all your heart."
Jeremiah 29:13

God has always been faithful to meet me when I have
taken time to seek Him. He has always given me extra
doses of His presence and blessings when I went out of
my way to seek Him. If you truly want more of Him, you
have to make time and not excuses. You will see the fruit
from it.

We can also meditate on His Word day and night
just like in Joshua 1:8, "Keep this Book of the Law
always on your lips; meditate on it day and night, so that
you may be careful to do everything written in it. Then
you will be prosperous and successful." Taking time to
read the Bible during those morning, afternoon and
evening times of prayer is a powerful way where God can
speak to us. The Word will not only encourage you and
lift you up, but it will also challenge you in areas that you
need to prune. When you hear the Word and do what it
says, you are truly loving Jesus and building a strong
foundation.

"Everyone then who hears these words of mine and does
them will be like a wise man who built his house on the
rock."
Matthew 7:24

Jesus also shows us the reason why we need to prune our own desires and obey what He says in the Word.

> "If you love me, keep my commands."
> John 14:15

We can easily run around saying, "I love you Lord", or "Jesus is my best friend", but if we are ignoring His word, we aren't loving Him at all. Some days when my kids misbehave repeatedly and they see how upset I am, they say "Sorry, I love you dad". I appreciate the apology, but I just want them to listen and obey, and not merely say they love me. Let's love Jesus by obeying Him.

We need to seek balance in everything we do. In our spiritual lives, if we only spend time praying and not reading the Word, we won't have the knowledge of His Word and will miss out when God wants to speak to us through it. If we only read and don't make time to pray, we will not develop an intimate relationship with God and be able to intercede for others. In our work lives, work must come with some rest. We can't only spend time at work and church, and then neglect to invest in our own family and households. Prune areas of your time to make room for balance. It's important to note that in addition to pruning and cutting out, we have to work at allowing God into everything that we do. It doesn't have to be a church activity, a ministry or prayer time for it to count towards something for God's glory.

"So whether you eat or drink or whatever you do, do it all for the glory of God."
1 Corinthians 10:31

Take a moment now to pray and ask God for guidance on what you should prune and where you should spend more of your time. Welcome back! Now fill in your time allocation goals on the next page of how you will spend your time going forward.

Time Allocation Goal

Work/School:

Social Media/Smartphone:

Family & Friends:

Exercise:

Rest:

Practice on Talent:

Hobbies:

Prayer:

Reading Bible:

Church:

Ministry/Volunteer/Charity:

Now, take out your calendar and start to pencil in certain activities for your week and month. Take a look at your day schedule for tomorrow and jot down how you plan to start your day and create a plan. For instance, if you've never prayed or read the Bible first thing in the morning, allocate ten minutes for tomorrow. Start small and work your way up. The same goes for exercise, practicing your talents, praying with your kids and sharing testimonies with them. Once you start developing these successful habits, there will be no stopping you. You will start to see the abundant fruit in your life and it will bless those around you.

Chapter 5

Pruning Sin

I got saved and starting following Jesus wholeheartedly when I was 17 years old. I was involved in various ministries and truly experienced the power of God in my life and in others. I definitely stumbled while in the race, but I never stopped heading towards the finish line. I came to a point in my life, before my fig tree revelation, that I knew I needed to re-commit my life to Him. Much like the stock market, my spiritual life was too volatile. I was tired of having really powerful moments in my life only to be shadowed by me hurting my testimony by dabbling in sinful things. I knew that I could never be perfect, but I was tired of being a hypocrite. My actions many times didn't match my words and it was a poor example of following Christ. We have God's grace to repent when we sin but that requires turning our back to that sin and not live in it. I believe that He gives us the power to not live in the same recurring sin. I was tired of going from lukewarm to hot and back in rapid cycles. So I went back to what kept my flame lit all these years, and that was my personal time in prayer and reading the Word. I started seeking the Kingdom first and it resulted in some major pruning.

"He cuts off every branch in me that bears no fruit,
while every branch that does bear fruit he prunes
so that it will be even more fruitful."
John 15:2

Social media is a very important aspect of our lives that needs pruning for two reasons. Not only for what can influence us but how we are influencing others. Social media is littered with sensual images and has gotten worse over the years. Even if you aren't following someone that posts those types of images, they are still suggested to you in certain sections of some apps. Sensual images and videos have become acceptable under certain guises like "health and fitness". I also started noticing lately that certain mainstream apps were starting to allow certain body parts to show that weren't allowed previously. It's the kind of stuff you don't want children to see. We are slowly being desensitized to this and it's producing triggers to lead believers into captivity. I know some people that have completely deleted these apps in order to avoid any kind of temptation. Some people might say that is extreme or that they should be strong enough to see the images and not be affected. But that goes against what the Bible says about temptation:

"Flee from sexual immorality"
1 Corinthians 6:18

Jesus also said:

"If your eye causes you to stumble, pluck it out. It is better for you to enter the kingdom of God with one eye than to have two eyes and be thrown into hell"
Mark 9:47

This is a strong metaphor on pruning and shows the importance of cutting away what causes us to sin. Don't go actually plucking your eyes out, but remove things that are causing you to fall into lust. Too many marriages are failing because of infidelity that started on social media. Even if social media doesn't lead you into physical adultery, it can still hurt a marriage or your walk with God. According to Jesus, adultery can happen with a look and a thought:

"But I tell you that anyone who looks at a woman lustfully has already committed adultery with her in his heart."
Matthew 5:28

I use social media pretty regularly for work, so my pruning started by unfollowing and by filtering. I unfollowed anyone that posted sensual images. There is also a way to click on "stop seeing images like this" on certain apps. This ended a lot of those images being suggested to me. Our relationships with God and our spouses are too important for us to have anything knock us off course. Sometimes we are the weakest at night when it comes to eating un-healthy or giving in to other temptations. For this reason, I know some folks that have pruned their late-night hours in order to get up earlier in the morning. These are simple adjustments we can make that can pay big dividends for living a victorious life.

Here comes the more difficult pill to swallow. How are we influencing people with our social media posts? Are our posts hurting our testimony and tainting people's view of Christianity? I can't tell you how many social media profiles I see with a Bible verse in the "About Me" section, praying hands and cross emojis, a bio saying "Jesus is my best friend", and then seeing images and videos from them displaying sensuality and drunkenness.

"Let us walk properly as in the daytime, not in orgies and drunkenness, not in sexual immorality and sensuality, not in quarreling and jealousy."
Romans 13:13

It's important that we don't cause others to sin since we are open letters to the world of what it means to be followers of Christ. We need to make sure we aren't hindering those from seeing His light in us. Whatever seeds you are planting on social media, that will be the type of harvest you will reap. The best advice I can give someone is to pause for five minutes before posting an image, video, political rant, joke, or any other type of post. Make sure it isn't going to water down your testimony, but, more importantly, see if that post is revealing to *you* where you are in your walk of faith. Those posts will reveal what you are focused on and what you are proud of. I'm pretty sure you know I'm not here to promote legalism with your wardrobe and that I'm not saying should only post scripture on your social media pages. Just make sure you are pruning your posts, align your actions with the Word and keep your testimony pure. My last piece of advice is to use discernment and check your sources before posting or sharing anything. I'm seeing a huge spike in believers sharing false prophecies, fake articles and quotes that were never said by the supposed author. Let's not muddy the water and confuse the world that is starving for hope and truth.

What other things in our lives cause us to sin? It may be a different thing for each one of us. There may be certain relationships that cause us to sin. It could be an activity that isn't sinful in nature, but may have triggers that cause us to sin (like getting excessively angry). Perhaps we need to prune the way we treat others. Sometimes in our love for the scriptures, we start becoming legalistic and extremely judgmental by forgetting the *spirit* of the law. We start to judge everyone with harsh measures, yet we neglect to remove the plank in our own eyes. Unforgiveness is another area that needs to be pruned and is often compared to a weed. It's a weed that can overpower us and hinder us from bearing fruit. Really give some thought to what is causing you to sin or triggering you throughout the day. Get to the root of it and prune it out of your life. Some of the sin I have pruned in the past sometimes tries to grow back in. We have to be diligent and stay on top of our pruning. It's a continuous process that will not end until we are in Heaven.

Chapter 6

Holding on to the Leaves

A few years after my fig tree experience, we moved to a new house in a new neighborhood. God revealed to me something different through a different tree. Our new property carried a different challenge in that we have many large trees and a bigger yard, which means, a lot more leaves to rake in the fall. My first fall in the new house, I decided to break up my raking into two separate rounds: Round one half-way through the fall and then round two once all the trees were bare. Round one was already overwhelming and I didn't look forward to the rest of the leaves falling for round two. Towards the end of the fall, I noticed that my neighbors' trees were bare and their yards were all nice and clean. I had one big tree in my front yard that was still full of leaves. I didn't want to do all the work of round two and then have this tree finally decide to let them fall. So I waited and hoped that snow wasn't in the near future that would bury the leaves in the yard until spring. A day of heavy rain came and I thought that the weight of the water would knock the leaves down, but nope. There they were, brown and frail but holding on. A week later, we had a really windy night and I was thrilled that I would wake up in the morning to a bare tree. Rise and shine! To my dismay, some leaves had been blown off but the tree was still pretty full. What was going on? I felt like the tree was teasing me. I started thinking to myself, "What is it with me and these trees?" That's when I realized that God was revealing something to me just like with the fig tree. Some of us have trouble letting go of the leaves that we need to prune. God sends the rain, the wind and the cold, but we are the tree that won't let go. You may have heard different messages at church or online, you may have felt the conviction when praying or reading the Bible, or perhaps this book has challenged a certain area of your life. I mentioned earlier in the book that you will have uncomfortable moments when reading this book and when you start pruning. It's not an easy process. You may be struggling to let go of certain sin and addictions in your life but you have to cut them out. There may be certain relationships that are causing you to continually fall into sin and it's tough to let those go or put on pause. It's hard to stop spending on things to fill your void, but it is hurting your financial future and impact on the Kingdom.

God called me to write his book and share how I pruned even the leaves off of the fig tree for it to bear abundant fruit and I didn't hesitate to prune the leaves off of my investments in order to please Him. If we now know what is underlying our investments and what we are profiting from, let's not hesitate to prune them, dive into biblically responsible investing, and trust in God and His provision in our lives. Remember, like it says in Psalm 24:1, "The earth is the LORD's, and everything in it, the world, and all who live in it." If God owns it all, and we are stewards of what He has entrusted to us, then let's be "all in." If all of us believers unite and prune our branches and leaves, we will have a tremendous impact on our world and for eternity. Prune your finances, your time, sin and any parts of your tree so that you can bear abundant fruit.

If you are strong in the Lord, continue on the path and let the pruning process allow you to bear even more fruit. If you have fallen away, there is no better time to re-commit your life to the Lord than right now. If you don't know Jesus as your Lord and Savior and want a relationship with Him, take a moment to pray right now. Accept Him and His sacrifice on the cross for you and the forgiveness of your sins. Repent of your sins and ask Him to guide your steps. Start to pray daily and read the Bible while asking for guidance and revelation. Pray for direction on finding a strong Bible-based church that embraces the full Gospel and get baptized. God will begin to prune you, as well as show you areas that need pruning, and you too will begin bearing fruit.

About the Author

Daniel Sciortino, ChFC® is a devoted husband and father of three children. He is a follower of Jesus Christ and active in his church and various charities. He was born in Argentina and his family migrated to America when he was two years old. His last name comes from his father's Sicilian roots. After graduating in 2001 from Rutgers University in New Jersey, he jumped right into the financial industry and never looked back.

As a financial planner and investment advisor at Fig Tree Wealth Management*, he enjoys working with his clients and guiding them into empowered stewardship. Biblically responsible investing is a passion of his and is making an impact on the world through it.

*Fig Tree Wealth Management is a division of National Wealth Management LLC

Quick Bible References

Biblically Responsible Investing

Proverbs 16:8

Deuteronomy 23:18

Blessings

2 Corinthians 9:8

Ecclesiastes 5:19

Contentment

Hebrews 13:5

Philippians 4:11-13

1 Timothy 6:6-12

Debt

Proverbs 22:7

Romans 13:8

Psalm 37:21

Diversification

Ecclesiastes 11:2

Giving

2 Corinthian 9:8-11

Luke 6:38

Matthew 6:20

Proverbs 11:25

Planning

Luke 14:28

Proverbs 15:22

Pruning

John 15:2

Prosperity

Joshua 1:8

Jeremiah 29:11

3 John 2

Saving & Investing

Matthew 25:14-30

Proverbs 13:11

Taxes

Mark 12:17

Tithing

Proverbs 3:9

Malachi 3:10

Time

Ephesians 5:15-17

Ecclesiastes 3:1-8

Work

Proverbs 14:23

Proverbs 6:10-11

1 Timothy 5:8

Colossians 3:23-24

Exodus 20:8-11

Your Personal Goals

1) How will you become a better steward of your finances?

2) How will you become a better steward of your time?

3) What sin and habits do you need to prune?

4) What charities do you plan on giving to of your time or money?

5) How can you be more effective at your current job?

6) Who can you pray for at your workplace?

7) Do you need to pray and consider a career change?

8) How can you better honor the Sabbath?

9) What else can you do to put the Kingdom first?

10) What investments can you prune for BRI?

Made in the USA
Middletown, DE
14 September 2020

19849833R00057